MW01518335

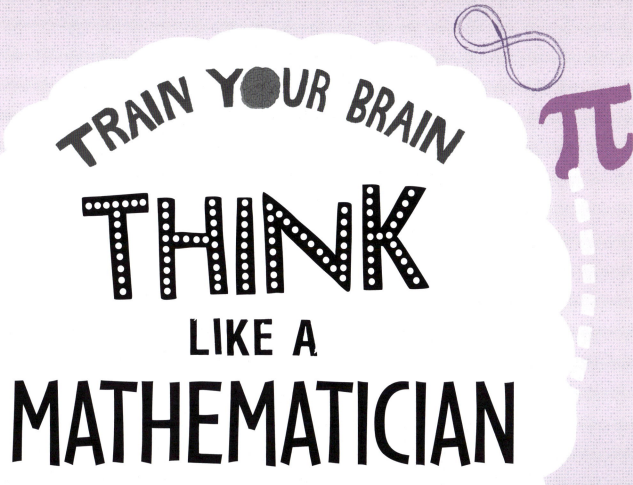

TRAIN YOUR BRAIN

THINK
LIKE A
MATHEMATICIAN

Written by Alex Woolf

Illustrated by David Broadbent

CRABTREE
PUBLISHING COMPANY
WWW.CRABTREEBOOKS.COM

CRABTREE
PUBLISHING COMPANY
WWW.CRABTREEBOOKS.COM

A note from the author and publisher
In preparation of this book, all due care has been exercised with regard to the instructions, activities, and techniques depicted. The publishers and author regret that they can accept no liability for any loss or injury sustained. Always get adult supervision and follow manufacturers' advice when using electric and battery-powered appliances.

The activities described in this book should always be done in the presence of a trusted adult. A trusted adult is a person (over 18 years old) in a child's life who makes them feel safe, comfortable, and supported. It might be a parent, teacher, family friend, care worker, or another adult.

Every effort has been made by the publishers to ensure websites are suitable for children, that they are of the highest educational value, and that they contain no inappropriate or offensive material. However, because of the nature of the Internet, it is impossible to guarantee that the contents of these sites will not be altered. We strongly advise that Internet access is supervised by a responsible adult.

Facts, figures, and dates were correct when going to press.

First published in Great Britain in 2021 by Wayland
Copyright © Hodder and Stoughton, 2021

Author: Alex Woolf
Illustrator: David Broadbent
Series editor: Melanie Palmer
Series design: David Broadbent
Editorial director: Kathy Middleton
Editor: Kathy Middleton
Proofreader: Crystal Sikkens
Production technician: Margaret Salter
Print coordinator: Katherine Berti

Library and Archives Canada Cataloguing in Publication
CIP available at Library and Archives Canada

Library of Congress Cataloging-in-Publication Data
CIP available at the Library of Congress

Crabtree Publishing Company

www.crabtreebooks.com   1-800-387-7650
Published by Crabtree Publishing Company in 2022.

Printed in the U.S.A./012022/CG20210915

Published in Canada
Crabtree Publishing
616 Welland Ave.
St. Catharines, Ontario
L2M 5V6

Published in the United States
Crabtree Publishing
347 Fifth Ave
Suite 1402-145
New York, NY 10016

CONTENTS

What Do Mathematicians Do?

Do you like to play around with numbers? Do you enjoy finding patterns in the things you look at? Then you could be a great mathematician!

Mathematicians study numbers, shapes, and quantities. They try to advance what we know about math by discovering new mathematical truths or laws. Some mathematicians work alone; others team up to solve problems together.

Like scientists, mathematicians are curious people. They ask themselves questions and develop theories, which they must try to prove. But mathematicians are not the same as scientists. Scientists prove their theories through experiments; mathematicians prove their theories using logic.

Mathematicians like to challenge themselves with difficult problems. They **persevere** because solving these problems is rewarding. They take risks and, like everyone, they sometimes make mistakes. That is part of how they learn.

Some mathematicians work only to advance human understanding of math. They are called pure mathematicians.

Others, called applied mathematicians, use what they know about math to help and support others. They might work with scientists, businesspeople, computer programmers, or engineers. A mathematician could, for example, help create a complex code that will make computers more secure, or they could help an astronomer calculate the distance from Earth to a star.

Do you like the sound of this kind of work? If so, read this book, and begin to train your brain to think like a mathematician.

Be Logical

To think like a mathematician, you need to use logic. Logic is the process of taking things you know and using them to deduce, or figure out, new things.

For example, here are two facts we know:
• Elsie likes all sports. • Soccer is a sport.
Using these facts, we can use logic to deduce a third fact:
• Elsie likes soccer.

I like soccer.

The facts of a logical argument, or discussion, are called the **premises**. Here are two premises:

1. All cats are mammals.

2. All mammals have warm blood.

From these premises, I can deduce:
3. My cat has warm blood.

This form of logic is called **deductive reasoning**. For it to work, the premises have to be true, and the conclusion you draw must be reasonable, or make sense. Look at the following statement:

1. Peter saw a crow on his way to school today.

2. Peter got into trouble at school.

Peter deduces: The crow caused him to get into trouble.

Can you see why the logic is wrong? Peter made a leap in logic he can't prove: He decided that seeing the crow caused him to get into trouble. But he probably saw a lot of things on the way to school. There's no direct connection to the bird. This is known as the "false cause **fallacy**." Don't fall for it!

Are any of the following statements not logical? If so, can you say why?

1. The Colosseum is a historic building in Rome, Italy.

2. Rome, Italy, is in Europe.

Conclusion: The Colosseum is in Europe.

1. Every time the rooster crows, the Sun rises.

2. When the Sun rises, the day begins.

Conclusion: The rooster causes the day to begin.

1. Cobras are a type of snake.

2. Cobras have venom that is deadly to humans.

Conclusion: All snakes are deadly to humans.

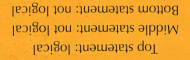

Top statement: logical
Middle statement: not logical
Bottom statement: not logical

Find the Proof

Mathematicians don't just accept facts because they seem right. They need to prove it. This makes a mathematician different from a jury in a court case.

If a lot of evidence points to a person's guilt, that's usually enough to prove them guilty beyond a reasonable doubt. But a mathematician would not call that proof.

Guilty!

Not proved!

If you have only ever seen white swans, you may reach the conclusion that all swans are white. This is a form of logic called **inductive reasoning**.

A mathematician would not accept that as proof. Just because you have never seen a black swan, it's not proof that black swans don't exist. This is why mathematicians always use deductive reasoning to prove something.

Mathematicians use deductive reasoning to develop proof that is true for all time and can never be not true. These kinds of proof are called **axioms**.

Mathematicians have already discovered many axioms. For example, we know that the **angles** in all triangles on a flat (not curved) surface add up to 180 degrees. We can use this knowledge to prove new things. So if we know two angles in a triangle, we can deduce the third.

Angle B is 90 degrees

Angle A is 45 degrees

Angle C is ?

The ancient Greek mathematician Euclid of Alexandria, who lived around 300 BCE, wrote down a collection of axioms, including the one above, in his famous book *The Elements*.

Think of a statement that you believe to be true, then see if you can prove it. Trying to prove something to yourself will help exercise your math brain.

Archimedes: Mathematician and Inventor

Born around 287 BCE, in Syracuse, Sicily (now a part of Italy), Archimedes was one of the greatest mathematicians who ever lived. He made important advances in pure mathematics. For example, he found a way of calculating the **area** of a circle. But he also used mathematics to solve practical problems.

King Hiero II of Syracuse ordered an enormous ship, the *Syracusia*, to be built. When it was completed, water was found to be leaking into the hull, and the ship's builders asked Archimedes for help. Archimedes's mathematical brain thought about what shapes might help raise water out of the boat. He pictured a hollow tube with a **spiral** inside it. When the tube's lower end was placed in the water, a handle at the top would be turned to make the spiral rotate. Water would be carried up the tube and out of the boat. The Archimedes Screw, as this invention was called, is still used today.

On another occasion, King Hiero II ordered a new crown. The king suspected that the goldsmith had only used some of the gold he had given him and mixed it with another metal for the crown, so he could keep the rest of the gold for himself. He asked Archimedes if he could figure out if his crown was pure gold.

Archimedes thought about this mathematically. A lump of pure gold that weighed the same as the crown should have the same **volume**. If the volume was different because a different metal was added, then this would prove that the crown was not pure gold. Archimedes first had to figure out how to measure the volume of an irregular shape, such as a crown.

Inspiration came while he was taking a bath. He noticed how the water in the tub overflowed when he got into it. He realized he could measure the crown's volume—or the volume of any irregularly shaped object—by placing it in water. The volume of water that overflowed would be the same volume as the crown. He was so excited, he ran out into the street shouting, *"Heurēka"* (or *eureka*), which is Greek for, "I have found it!"

During his lifetime, Archimedes used his mathematical skills to solve many practical problems. He discovered how levers and pulleys can be used to help move heavy objects easily. When the Romans besieged Syracuse, he invented war machines to help defend the city. Archimedes died around 212 BCE. He was working on a mathematical problem and didn't even realize the Romans had captured Syracuse. It is said that when a Roman soldier arrived to arrest him, he refused to go with him and the enraged soldier killed him.

Solve Problems

Mathematicians love trying to solve math problems. It can take a lot of patience and hard work, but solving a problem is one of the most satisfying parts of a mathematician's work.

If I give you 1.75 oz (50 g) of food a day, how much do you eat in a week?

Of course, math is also about learning the rules, such as how you multiply and divide numbers. You learn these in your math lessons at school. But the really fun part is when you start to use these rules to solve practical problems.

Math problems are all around us. To start thinking like a mathematician, why don't you look for math problems the next time you go out somewhere. See if you can figure out how to solve them.

✹ When you're in the supermarket, try figuring out the price of four cans of baked beans.

1 can costs 54 cents, so 4 cans cost...

✹ When you're in a car, figure out how long it will take you to reach your destination based on your current speed.

✹ If you're saving up to buy something, figure out how much you earn from doing chores around the house. Then calculate how long it will take you to save the money you need.

✹ When you're cooking, figure out how long the chicken needs to be in the oven based on its weight.

✹ Here's a problem you can try. Imagine you are packing to go on vacation. You pack five T-shirts and three pairs of shorts.

How many T-shirt/shorts combinations will this give you?

Answer: 15 T-shirt/shorts combinations

Think Visually

When someone says the word "apple" to you, what happens? Do you see an apple in your head? This is called thinking visually. As mathematicians, we need to learn how to start thinking visually about math problems.

Visual mathematics means working with shapes and pictures rather than numbers. Many mathematicians like to think and work in this way. For example, Maryam Mirzakhani (1977–2017), one of the greatest of modern mathematicians, worked almost entirely visually. She sketched her ideas on large pieces of paper.

If you're struggling for an answer when working purely with numbers, you can sometimes see the answer to the problem more easily by thinking visually.

Here are some exercises to help you practice thinking visually about math.

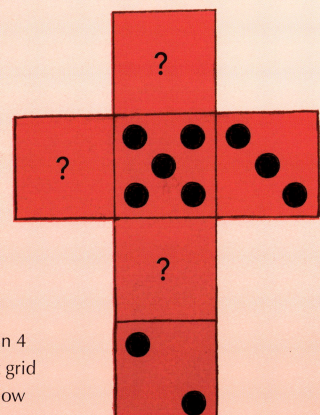

1. Imagine you're going to fold up this shape to make a die. How many spots should be on each of the empty faces? Here's a tip: the spots on the opposite faces must add up to 7.

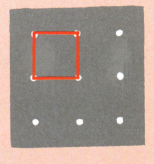

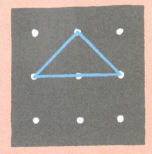

2. In your mind, join 4 dots on this nine-dot grid to make a shape. How many shapes can you make? How many of them are triangles and how many are quadrilaterals (4-sided shapes)?

3. Using your visual imagination, find the missing line to turn each of these shapes into a square and two triangles.

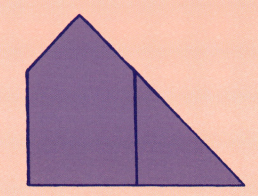

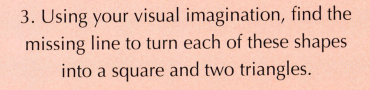

Investigate Numbers

Numbers are all around us. How many minutes will your walk take? How many people are ahead of you in a line? How much is your shopping bill going to be? To think like mathematicians, we should get into the habit of counting and measuring things.

It's fun to estimate the quantity of something first and then do a count to see how close you were. For example, try guessing how many books are on your bookshelf. Then guess how many of those books you've read. Was the **proportion** of books you've read bigger or smaller than you guessed?

What do we do with these measurements once we have them? We can make them interesting and useful if we compare them to other similar measurements, and then turn the results into a graph.

For example, you could make a graph showing the time it takes you to walk to school taking a slightly different route each day. The graph will tell you the quickest route.

Try doing a **survey** of your friends' favorite fruits. See which fruit gets the most votes.

Be a math detective. Follow the clues and identify the secret number in the list below.

47   24   35   58   15   73   9   130   99   13   37

Clues:

- the secret number has two digits
- both digits are odd
- the digit in the tens place is lower than the digit in the ones place
- the ones digit is not lower than four
- the sum of the two digits is a multiple of four

Answer: 35

Emmy Noether: Overcoming Prejudice

Emmy Noether is regarded by many as the most important woman in the history of mathematics. She was born in 1882 to a German Jewish family. In those days, girls were expected to focus on arts subjects rather than science or mathematics. Noether studied at first to be a language teacher, but in 1900 she decided to follow her real passion—mathematics.

At the University of Erlangen, she was one of just two female mathematics students out of thousands of men. In 1907, she completed her Ph.D. She faced **prejudice** because she was a woman, and she couldn't get a job in her field. So she worked at the university without pay for seven years.

Despite this, her reputation grew. In 1915, she was invited by colleagues to join the mathematics department at the University of Göttingen. Even then, the university refused to give her a salary or position, and she lectured, or taught, for four years under the name of a male colleague.

In 1918, Noether developed a mathematical proof known as Noether's theorem. This became one of the most important mathematical theorems of the 20th century. It helps explain things like gravity and ocean waves. It is used by scientists to predict weather patterns, nuclear explosions, and the vibrations of bridges.

In 1919, Noether was finally given an official position at the University of Göttingen. Her reputation in mathematical circles continued to flourish. She visited other universities and conferences giving lectures. In 1932, she received a major award in mathematics.

Noether's skill as a mathematician was to see connections between different things and find rules to explain them. She thought about ideas rather than just about numbers. She also loved solving problems. Her classes at Göttingen became famous because she would never use lesson plans. Instead she would encourage her students to discuss difficult mathematical problems. These discussions were so groundbreaking that some of her students used their notes from these classes to write books on the mathematical problems they had discussed.

In 1933, the Nazi Party came to power in Germany and Jews were no longer allowed to hold university positions. Noether left Germany and moved to the U.S.A. Sadly, she died in 1935, at age 53. Noether remains an inspiring figure in mathematics because she had to battle prejudice throughout her life, yet still managed to achieve so much.

University of Göttingen

Try Working Backward

Math problems can be quite tricky. Part of being a mathematician is finding creative ways to tackle problems. Sometimes, the hardest part is figuring out where to start. If you're struggling, one approach you might try is to work backward!

Working backward means starting with the solution and then working back one step at a time to get to the beginning.

This is a method we often use in our ordinary lives. For example, when figuring out how to get somewhere, it's often easier to think about the destination first and then work backward to your starting point.

We can take the same approach with a mathematics problem. Here's an example:

In the morning, Dad left a bowl of candies on the kitchen table. In the course of the day, Joe ate 4, Vicky ate 2, and she gave 3 to each of her two friends. At the end of the day, there were 6 candies left in the bowl. How many were there to begin with?

Remember that each calculation must be reversed when you work backward. If you add when you work forward, you have to subtract if you work backward. If you multiply working forward, then you must divide when working backward.

During the day the candies were taken away, or subtracted, from the bowl. But in our calculation we're working backward to get to the original number, so the candies must be put back, or added. So, starting with the number of candies left in the bowl, can you add all the candies that were taken to arrive at the original number?

Answer: 18

Mistakes Are Okay!

Math is the kind of subject where answers tend to be either right or wrong. However, that doesn't mean making mistakes is a sign of failure. Mistakes are a vital part of how we learn math.

So don't feel frustrated or foolish when you make a mistake. See it as an opportunity to develop a deeper understanding of the problem you're trying to tackle.

Fear of making mistakes might lead us to avoid answering difficult math problems. But rather than leave it blank, give it a try. Your answer may be wrong, but you'll have learned something in the process. For one thing, you'll learn what doesn't work.

Let's look at it another way: if you're not making any mistakes in your math problems, that's a sign that they are too easy for you and you should probably be working on more advanced problems. Making mistakes is a sign that you're being challenged—in other words, you're working at the right level.

The next time you make a mistake, take the time to understand why your answer is wrong. Go back to the question and look hard at everything you did. You may find you made a simple error that threw everything out, or that your math was good but you didn't fully understand the question to begin with. If you still can't figure it out, ask your teacher for help.

If you make the effort to discover the reason for your error, the knowledge will stay in your brain and you'll remember how to do it right the next time.

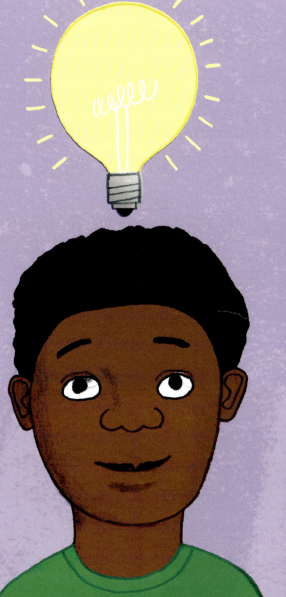

Look For Patterns

Math is full of fascinating and mysterious patterns.
A pattern in math can be a **sequence** of numbers
or shapes that repeats, or a sequence put in order
according to a rule.

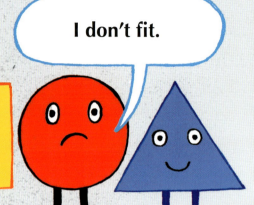

I don't fit.

To think like a mathematician, try to discover these patterns. When faced with
a mathematical puzzle, such as a series of numbers that you need to continue,
ask yourself if there is a pattern. For example:

1   4   7   10   13   16

This sequence has a difference of 3 between each number.

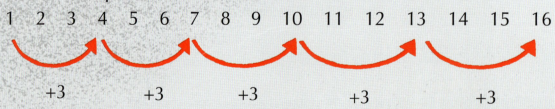

Now try to figure out the pattern in this sequence of numbers:

1   7   13   19   25   x

What should x be?

Answer: 31

Pascal's Triangle is an interesting number pattern that you can build yourself.

Look carefully at the triangle of squares below. It's known as Pascal's Triangle, named for the French mathematician Blaise Pascal, who studied it. You'll notice that each square contains a number that is the sum of the two squares directly above it. (If there is only one square above it, it simply repeats that number.)

Copy the triangle onto another sheet of paper. We've included the first four rows. See if you can fill out the rest of them.

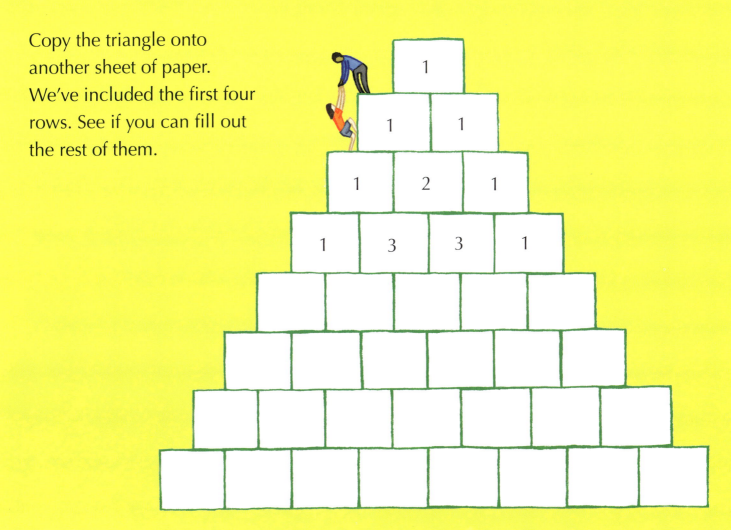

Once it's filled in, look carefully at the numbers in Pascal's Triangle and see what patterns you can find. Try adding up each row of the triangle. Is there a pattern in the sums of the numbers? Now try adding up the diagonals. Again, you should see a pattern.

Terence Tao: The Great Collaborator

Born in 1975, Terence Tao is an Australian-American mathematician of Chinese heritage, and is considered by many to be the finest mathematician of his generation. As a child, Tao showed a remarkable talent for the subject and was studying university-level math courses by the age of nine.

A year later, he became the youngest ever participant in the International Mathematical Olympiad, where he won a bronze medal. Three years later, he won gold. Tao earned a university degree at age 16 and received his Ph.D. at 21. In 1999, at 24, he became a full professor at the University of California.

Tao's most famous achievement in math was the Green-Tao theorem, which he developed with British mathematician Ben Green. They were concerned with a set of numbers called primes: numbers that can only be divided by themselves and 1. For example, the numbers 2, 3, 5, and 7 are all prime numbers.

Some prime numbers are equally spaced (e.g. 3, 7, and 11 are 4 spaces apart). These equally spaced strings of prime numbers can be quite long. The Green-Tao theorem proves that no matter how long these strings of prime numbers might get, there will always be another string that is longer.

Terence Tao loves to collaborate with other mathematicians. He has worked with dozens of colleagues in the course of making his discoveries and is constantly learning from them. He understands that to tackle the really hard problems, it helps to combine your talents with others, since no single mathematician can be a master of the entire subject. Working together is a key skill that can suit some mathematicians or math problems, but it takes practice and good listening skills.

This was the case with the Green-Tao theorem. Not only did Green and Tao collaborate with each other, they also made use of work done by earlier mathematicians.

Tao believes that mathematics should be about communicating your ideas and making connections with the work of other mathematicians. He is constantly blogging about his projects, celebrating the achievements of others, and sharing new ideas. He's happy when someone points out an error in his calculations because it helps him to improve his theories.

Tao views math problems as opponents—very cunning opponents—and his job is to try and see a way through their defenses.
He is humble enough to realize that these opponents can't be defeated by one person alone.
It takes many minds, and sometimes generations, to achieve victory.

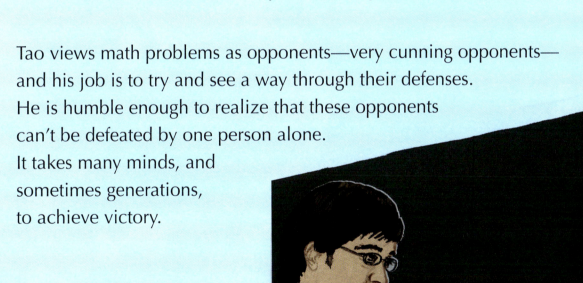

$$+ \, o(1)) \, \frac{N^2}{(\log N)^k}$$

Play Games

One great way to build up your math skills is by playing games. Many of the card, board, and video games you play involve juggling numbers. Because you're so busy having fun, you often don't even realize you're also training your brain to be a mathematician.

In the card game called 21, the winner is the player whose cards add up closest to 21, but no higher. In this game, jacks, queens, and kings are worth 10, and an ace is worth 1 or 11—it's your choice.

First, each player is dealt two cards. They can either keep just those two cards or ask for a third card in an attempt to be the closest player to 21. This can be a tricky decision. If you have a 10 and a 7, another card might take you close or equal to 21—great!—or put you over 21—you lose!

Playing 21 not only improves your adding skills, it also helps you think about chance. You know what numbers you need, and you have to figure out the chances of being dealt the right card.

Looking at the cards that have been played, you'll need to calculate what cards are still available. For example, if two aces have been played already, what are the chances of picking another ace? If there are a lot of cards left in the pile, the chance is low, but if there are only a few cards left, then the chance is higher.

Why not try entering a math competition?

The International Mathematical Olympiad is the Olympic Games of mathematics. Every year, students from more than a hundred countries compete against each other by trying to solve math problems within a time limit. Competitions like this encourage you to think quickly and accurately under pressure, which is great training to help build a mathematical brain.

Work Systematically

With tricky math problems, it helps to work with a plan in mind. This is called working systematically. You can work without a plan, but it usually ends up taking a lot longer.

Time's up!

Working systematically means not diving into a problem right away. It means taking a moment to think about whether there's a simpler, less time-consuming way of solving it.

Here's an example. You're given a series of numbers: 4, 7, 11, 12, 17, and 24.

You're asked which of these numbers is a multiple of 2. You could just dive in and start dividing every number by two. Or you could save yourself time by remembering that multiples of 2 are always even numbers. Now you know you only have to divide the even numbers by two.

Working systematically doesn't just help you with math, but also with other problems you face in your schoolwork or your life. A good rule is to think before you act. Try coming up with different options before deciding on the best solution.

Try out this problem:

Your coat has three buttons and you want to do it up. You could start with the bottom button, the top button, or the middle button.

How many ways can you find to do up your coat? By working systematically, you'll have a better chance of finding all of them.

Now try the same with a four-button coat. Based on what you've learned, can you predict the number of ways you can do up a coat with five buttons or six buttons?

Here's a game you can try:

Start with a target number of 23.

Player 1 chooses a number between 1 and 4.
Player 2 then chooses a number between 1 and 4 and adds it to Player 1's number.

Continue choosing numbers by taking turns.
The player that first hits the target of 23 wins.

Can you find a system for winning this game? Does it help to go first or not?

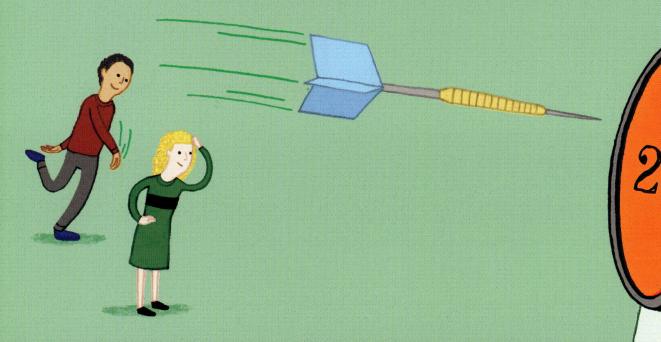

Find the General Rule

Mathematics is full of general rules. For example, a triangle with three equal sides will always have three equal angles, no matter how big or small it is. To think like a mathematician, always look for the general rule.

In many ways, we're the same.

Let's look at odd and even numbers. Take any two odd numbers and add them together. Is the answer even? Will it always be even? Can you figure out why this is? Drawing a picture of a sum can sometimes make the reason for the general rule clearer.

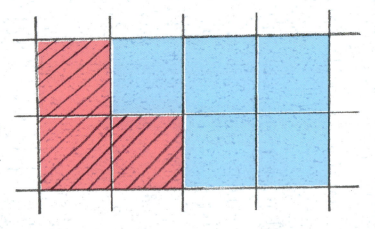

Now take any odd number and any even number and multiply them together. Is the answer even? Will it always be even? Why do you think this is? Here's a clue: an even number is any number that can be divided by 2 (and the result is a whole number).

There are also general rules for **square numbers**. A square number is the product of a number multiplied by itself. Here is a sequence of square numbers:

$$1 \times 1 = 1$$

$$2 \times 2 = 4$$

$$3 \times 3 = 9$$

Can you see anything interesting in the sequence 1, 4, 9? The pattern is odd, even, odd. Do you think the next square number will be even? Why is this?

To answer this, it may help to draw it as a picture:

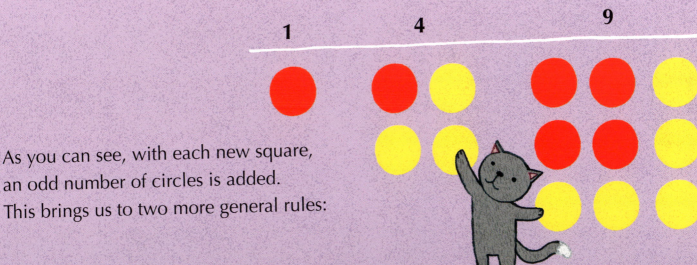

As you can see, with each new square, an odd number of circles is added. This brings us to two more general rules:

Any odd number plus any odd number = an even number
Any odd number plus any even number = an odd number

As you can see, math is full of general rules.

Please note: on pages 32–33, when it says "numbers," it always means whole numbers, not fractions or decimals.

Be Resilient

Good mathematicians are resilient. This means they work hard and don't give up easily when faced with a challenging problem. When they fail—and we all fail sometimes—they dust themselves off and try again with a different approach.

To develop your resilience, why not challenge yourself with some tricky math problems. Try this maze puzzle.

Go through the maze adding up all the numbers you pass. What's the lowest total number you can make going through the maze? What is the highest total?

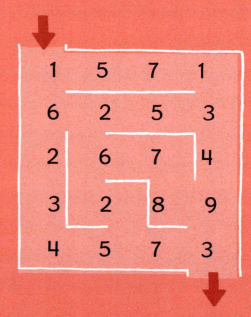

On a digital clock the time sometimes shows **consecutive** numbers, either going forward or backward. Some examples are 6:54, 2:34, 10:11. Figure out how many times there are consecutive numbers in a 12-hour clock.

Cut a square into four triangles and see how many shapes you can make from them. You can only fit long sides to long sides and short sides to short sides.

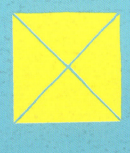
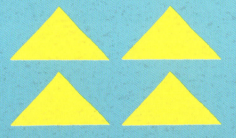

Take four pairs of socks. Mix them up so all the pairs are mismatched. Make sure that no mismatched pair is the same as another mismatched pair. Is there more than one way of doing this?

The solutions to some of the math problems you'll face may not be obvious right away. Sometimes you'll have to struggle to solve them. Try to be resilient, because when you do solve them, success will taste so much sweeter!

Sofya Kovalevskaya: Trailblazer

Sofya Kovalevskaya (born Sofya Korvin-Krukovskaya) was born in Russia in 1850, and grew up to be a pioneer for women in mathematics. She was the first woman to earn a **doctorate** in the subject, the first female professor in northern Europe, and one of the first women to edit a mathematics journal.

Her interest in mathematics began at an early age. When she was 11, due to a shortage of wallpaper, her father covered her bedroom wall with his old mathematics notes. Sofya studied these with interest. She further developed her mathematical brain by borrowing a book on **algebra** and reading it in bed at night. At the age of 14, she taught herself trigonometry (the mathematics of triangles). Her tutor noticed her remarkable talent and urged her father to allow her to continue her education.

Sofya wanted to study mathematics at university, but the only universities open to women were in Europe. Even there, women could not enroll as students, but they could attend lectures. Since young, unmarried women weren't allowed to travel alone, Sofya married a man named Vladimir Kovalevsky for the purpose of being able to travel freely. In 1869, Sofya and Vladimir traveled to Heidelberg, Germany.

In 1870, Sofya Kovaleveskaya moved to Berlin, where she managed to impress Karl Weierstrass, a famous mathematician, with her math skills. He agreed to tutor her. She studied under Weierstrass for four years and produced three papers, which earned her a doctorate in mathematics.

Kovaleveskaya continued to work hard on her mathematics. She wrote and presented papers, one of which won a prize from the French Academy of Science. In 1883, she took a job as a lecturer at the University of Stockholm in Sweden. The following year she became the editor of a mathematics journal. She even found time to co-write a play. Sadly, in 1891, Kovaleveskaya died at the young age of 41 after falling ill with pneumonia.

During her career, Sofya Kovalevskaya published ten papers in mathematics, many of which were groundbreaking and inspired future discoveries. Not only was she a great mathematician, she was also a talented writer and a campaigner for women's rights. It was in part thanks to her struggle to obtain a university education that more universities began to open their doors to women.

Put In the Practice

The more math you do, the quicker you'll become at being able to figure out math problems. Math problems are often simple **operations** disguised in unmathematical language. The more you do, the better you will get at seeing through the disguise.

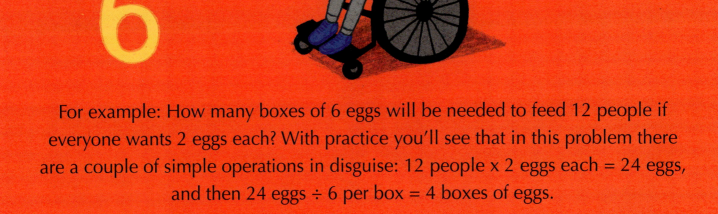

I see you!

For example: How many boxes of 6 eggs will be needed to feed 12 people if everyone wants 2 eggs each? With practice you'll see that in this problem there are a couple of simple operations in disguise: 12 people x 2 eggs each = 24 eggs, and then 24 eggs ÷ 6 per box = 4 boxes of eggs.

To answer the problem above without a calculator, you need to know your times tables. Spending time learning these by memory can save a huge amount of time when you do math problems.

You might find yourself struggling with certain operations, such as subtraction or division. If these take you longer or you're still making a few mistakes, focus on doing these kinds of problems. Time yourself and see if you can improve your speed and accuracy.

Your brain is like a muscle that needs training to grow in strength. The more math problems you do, the faster you'll get at these simple but important skills of adding, subtracting, multiplying, and dividing.

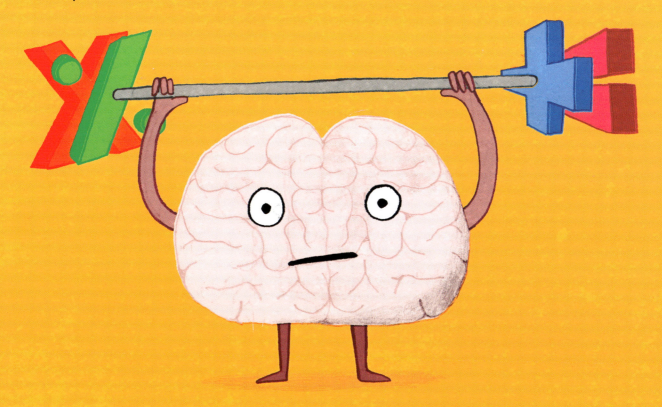

Here's a great math warm-up exercise:

Pick any number and think of 10 ways you can reach that number. For example, if you picked 16, you could say: 12 + 4, 4 x 4, 19 - 3, 32 ÷ 2, and so on.

It's easy, but if you do it a lot, it will help you speed up your basic skills.

Think About Chance

In math, we can usually predict, or guess, whether an answer will be right or wrong. If you add an apple to a bowl that contains 4 apples, the bowl will always end up with 5 apples. But mathematicians are also interested in the likelihood of something happening, or its **probability**. This needs a different kind of math.

It might land in there or it might not!

If you toss a coin 100 times, it's probable that around half the time it will land on tails and half the time on heads. But it's not certain. It's possible it might land on tails every time, although very unlikely.

Probability is useful to mathematicians because the world around us isn't certain. There are many things we can't predict with 100 percent accuracy, such as the weather. Probability helps us to figure out the likelihood of something, such as whether it will rain, so we can plan for it.

Probability is shown as a fraction. Below, Amy has 4 blue balls, 5 red balls, and 3 green balls. She puts them all into a bag and picks one out at random. What is the probability that she will pick a blue ball? To figure this out, divide the number of blue balls by the total number of balls. The answer is $\frac{4}{12}$ or $\frac{1}{3}$.

Higher Number Wins

Here's a game you can play using probability and strategy, or planning: Two players each draw a row of 4 boxes. They take turns rolling a die, and the roller must decide in which of the boxes to place the number he or she has rolled. They each roll the die 4 times until the boxes are filled. The player with the higher 4-digit number wins.

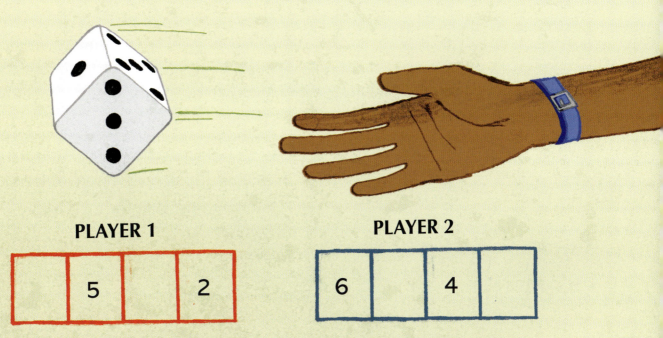

PLAYER 1

	5		2

PLAYER 2

6		4	

Work Together

Math can be great fun when working as a team, with a partner, or in a small group. It can also be useful when working on a difficult problem that requires different skills. We all have unique strengths and often several brains are better than one.

Working as a team on a math problem is not always easy. Some people may be louder than others or more eager to speak. That doesn't necessarily mean they have the best ideas. Make sure that everyone gets a chance to speak—and not all at once!

Let each person, in turn, offer their thoughts on a problem. Once all ideas have been shared, you can reach a decision together on the most likely solution.

Here is a math game that's great for working on as a team.

Dice in the Corner

Line up three dice in a corner so only 7 faces are visible. The only rule is that, where two faces touch, they must be the same number. As a team, figure out what the missing faces show. Remember: opposite faces always add up to 7.

Here's another fun teamwork challenge:

Guess the Game Tokens

One person in the group (the designer) arranges a row of different colored game tokens, keeping the row hidden from the others so they cannot see it. The other members of the team ask the designer questions to try to figure out how they are arranged. The designer can only answer "yes" or "no."

Here are examples of the kinds of questions you can ask:

- Are there more than four tokens?

- Are there any red tokens?

- Are the blue tokens touching?

- Is the design **symmetrical**?

- Are there two tokens to the left of the yellow token?

See if, working as a team, you can guess the design with 20 questions or less.

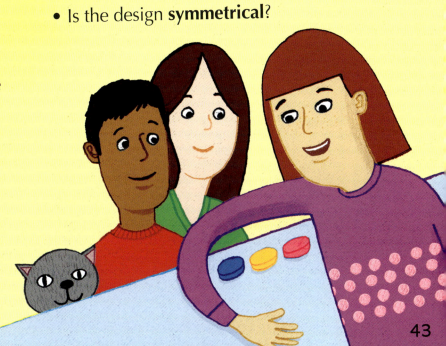

Math Is Everywhere

Math is an important tool we use to help us understand the world around us. You couldn't cook, shop, tell time, or play a board game without some understanding of numbers. Even when you're planting seeds in the garden, you're measuring the depth of the soil and counting how many seeds you need.

Engineers need math to build the machines we use, including computers, cars, and phones. Architects use **geometry** to design buildings; meteorologists use mathematical models to predict the weather; astronauts use math to move around in space; and musicians use math to compose and play music.

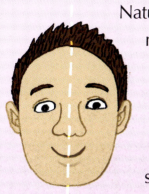

Nature is full of
mathematical patterns,
such as the symmetry
of your face or the ripples that
spread when you throw a
stone into a pond. As a mathematician, you will
study the rules that shape everything—including yourself.

Try thinking more about the numbers around you. Take the time to measure and compare things. Keep working on those math problems, and don't worry if you make mistakes. The most important thing is to have fun with numbers!

Now that you've read this book, you've got all the information you need to start thinking like a mathematician. So don't delay any longer. The world of mathematics is waiting for you.

Glossary

algebra A branch of mathematics in which letters and other symbols are used to represent numbers in problems

angles The amount of space between intersecting lines close to the point where they meet

area The measurement of a surface

axioms Mathematical statements that have been established as true for all time

consecutive Items following one another in order

deductive reasoning Using known facts to reach a conclusion

doctorate The highest degree awarded by a university

fallacy A mistake in reasoning

geometry A branch of mathematics that deals with measurement, lines, and angles

inductive reasoning Using things learned from experience and observation to reach a general conclusion about something

logic Taking facts and using them to deduce new things

operations Mathematical processes, such as addition, subtraction, multiplication, and division

persevere To continue on even in the face of failure or obstacles

prejudice An unfair feeling of dislike or hatred for a person or group

premises Statements that form the basis of a logical argument

probability The likeliness that an event will occur

proportion The relationship of one thing to another in terms of quantity, size, or number

sequence A series of something, such as numbers

spiral A continuous curve around a central line, like a screw

square numbers Numbers that are the product of a number multiplied by itself

survey An investigation into the views of a group of people

symmetrical Describing something made up of two identical, mirrored halves

volume The amount of space occupied by a 3-D object

Further Information

Books

Go Figure! (series). Steve Mills, Hilary Koll, and Anne Rooney. Crabtree Publishing, 2015-16.
This series encourages you to use real data and fascinating facts to solve mathematical problems. There are titles on space, extreme sports, computer games, the human body, the animal kingdom, the ocean, and planet Earth.

Math on the Job (series). Richard Wunderlich. Crabtree Publishing, 2016.
This series reveals how much math is an integral part of high-interest careers in business, marine animal care, health care, community service, construction, and sports.

Fantasy Baseball Math. Allan Morey. Capstone Press, 2016.
Young baseball fans will get a kick out of learning about the basic math skills behind baseball statistics.

Websites

www.mathsisfun.com/
This huge website is packed full of explanations, examples, games, puzzles, activities, and worksheets to engage all age levels.

www.pbslearningmedia.org/resource/mkaet.math.sp.baseball/real-life-math-baseball/
In this video, an assistant general manager from a MLB (Major League Baseball) team explains the role of statistics and other math in team operations.

http://mathcentral.uregina.ca/beyond/articles/medicine/med1.html
This Math Central link gives examples to show how doctors, nurses, and other healthcare professionals use math.

http://mathcentral.uregina.ca/beyond/articles/Architecture/ConstructionANDDesign.html
This Math Central link explores how math is used in construction and design.

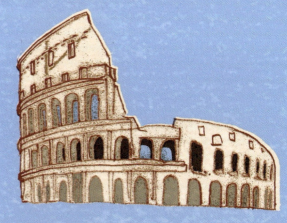

Index